Flavo

DERB

RECIPES

Compiled by Julia Skinner

THE FRANCIS FRITH COLLECTION

www.francisfrith.com

First published in the United Kingdom in 2011 by The Francis Frith Collection®

This edition published exclusively for Identity Books in 2011 ISBN 978-1-84589-574-7

Text and Design copyright The Francis Frith Collection®
Photographs copyright The Francis Frith Collection® except where indicated.

British Library Cataloguing in Publication Data

Flavours of Derbyshire - Recipes
Compiled by Julia Skinner

The Francis Frith Collection
Oakley Business Park,
Wylye Road, Dinton,
Wiltshire SP3 5EU
Tel: +44 (0) 1722 716 376
Email: info@francisfrith.co.uk
www.francisfrith.com

Printed and bound in Malaysia

Front Cover: **BUXTON, THE CAT AND FIDDLE 1914** 67581p
Frontispiece: **CHESTERFIELD, STEPHENSON PLACE 1914** 67563

The colour-tinting is for illustrative purposes only, and is not intended to be historically accurate

CONTENTS

CASTLETON, SPEEDWELL CAVERN
1909 61785

(or mi...
450g/1 lb onion...
Chopped fresh parsley, to taste
Chopped fresh thyme, to taste
Salt and pepper, to taste
300ml/½ pint stock

Pre-heat the oven to 190°C/375°F/Gas Mark 5.
Dice the meat, and peel and slice the onions. Layer the meat and
onions alternately in an ovenproof casserole dish, then sprinkle on
the herbs and seasoning, to taste.

Pour over the stock, cover the casserole dish with its lid and cook
in the pre-heated oven for at least 2 hours, or until the meat is well
cooked and tender. When ready to serve, the gravy can be thickened
with a little flour or cornflour if necessary.

MONSAL DALE, THE VIADUCT c1955 M221005

3

RECIPE

PEAK DISTRICT SPRING LAMB WITH DERBYSHIRE HONEY GLAZE

For centuries Derbyshire has been a famous sheep farming a ram appears on the coat of arms of Derbyshire County Co lamb reared on the heather moors and upland hill farms o District is particularly famous for its quality and flavour. I a joint of fine Peak District spring lamb is teamed with D honey, ginger and rosemary to give a spicy gloss to th residue left in the roasting tin makes a delicious grav moorlands are thick with wild flowers and heather i busy bees turn into delicious honey. There are a nu honey producers in the county, as well as smaller – look out for local honey at good food shops ar throughout Derbyshire.

1.5-2kg/3-4 lbs joint of Peak District spri
Salt and pepper
1 teaspoonful ground ginger
1 dessertspoonful dried rosemary
2 good tablespoonfuls runny Derb
300ml/ ½ pint dry cider

t the oven to 200°C/400°F/Ga
epper and ginger, the
he rosemary a
rou

RECIPE

FIDGETY PIE

This is the Derbyshire version of the hearty and flavoursome 'fidget' or 'fitchett' pies that are found in several parts of England. They were traditionally made at harvest time, either to feed the harvesters working in the fields or to welcome them home when they had finished their day's work – the key ingredients of apples and onions are fresh and plentiful at this time of the year. One theory for the unusual name is that 'fitched' meant five-sided, and the pies may originally have been made in a five-sided shape. However, another interpretation is that 'fitchett' was an old name for a pole-cat; as polecats are known for their strong smell, the name may originally have been a light-hearted comment on the strong aroma that filled the kitchen as these pies were cooking. However, they taste delicious! This pie can be eaten either hot or cold.

  300g/10oz shortcrust pastry
  2 medium onions, peeled and thinly sliced
  1 large cooking apple, peeled, cored and thinly sliced
  3 medium-sized potatoes
  1 dessertspoonful finely chopped fresh sage leaves
    (or 1 teaspoonful chopped dried sage)
  Salt and pepper to taste
  150ml/5 fl oz/¼ pint beef or vegetable stock
  1 dessertspoonful oil
  225g/8oz bacon rashers, de-rinded and cut into pieces
  25g/1oz sultanas or raisins
  A little milk or beaten egg, to glaze the pastry

Pre-heat the oven to 180°C/350°F/Gas Mark 4. Grease a large pie dish or baking tin.

Bring a pan of lightly salted water to the boil. Peel the potatoes and add to the pan. Cook in boiling water for 15 minutes, then drain and cut the potatoes into thin slices.

Heat the oil in a large frying pan and fry the bacon pieces until they are cooked through, then remove from the pan. Add the sliced onions to the pan and cook gently until they are soft and transparent.

Roll out two-thirds of the pastry to about 5mm (¼ inch) thick and use it to line the greased pie dish or tin. Put half the sliced potatoes in the bottom of the dish. Cover with a layer of half the sliced apples, then a layer of half the onions. Sprinkle over the chopped sage, then season with pepper and a little salt – you don't need to add much salt, as the bacon will make the dish salty. Add the bacon pieces, and sprinkle with the sultanas. Cover with a layer of the remaining sliced potatoes, then the remaining onions, and season lightly again. Finish off with a layer of the rest of the apples. Pour the stock over the filling. Dampen the pastry rim, then roll out the remaining pastry to make a lid for the pie about 5mm (¼ inch) thick. Pinch the pastry edges together firmly to seal them well, and trim the edges. Cut a cross in the centre of the lid to allow steam to escape during cooking, and brush the lid with a little milk or beaten egg, to glaze.

Bake in the centre of the pre-heated oven for 40 minutes, then reduce the oven temperature to 150°C/300°F/Gas Mark 2 and bake for a further 40-45 minutes. Check after 20 minutes – if the pastry is browning too much, cover the pie with foil for the rest of the cooking time, to prevent it burning.

HAYFIELD, MOUNT FAMINE, KINDER c1960 H298010

This shows the open hill area known as Mount Famine in the Peak District near Hayfield. Its curious name derives from the fact that no crops would grow there.

RECIPE

MEDLEY PIE

A medley pie was a savoury pie made with a combination of ingredients, a 'medley' of left-over cooked meats. This is a Derbyshire recipe for medley pie, where it is flavoured with sage and onions.

> 225g/8oz shortcrust pastry
> 225g/8oz lean bacon rashers, de-rinded
> 350g/12oz left-over pieces of cooked meat, such as beef, lamb, rabbit, chicken, pork
> 1 onion
> 1 dessertspoonful finely chopped fresh sage leaves (or one teaspoonful dried chopped sage)
> 1 egg, beaten
> Salt and pepper to taste
> 300ml/ ½ pint brown stock
> A little fat or oil for frying

Pre-heat the oven to 190°C/375°F/Gas Mark 5.

Cut the bacon into pieces, and peel and chop the onion. Heat a little fat or oil in a pan, and fry the onion with the bacon until soft, then put into an ovenproof pie dish together with the meat that is being used. Sprinkle over the sage and seasoning to taste, and pour over the stock.

Roll out the pastry on a floured surface. Place the pastry over the pie, seal to the rim of the pie dish and trim the edges. Make a slit in the centre of the pastry lid to allow steam to escape. Brush the pastry with the beaten egg to glaze, then bake in the pre-heated oven for about 1 hour, until the pastry is crisp and golden brown.

RECIPE

MEDLEY PIE

A medley pie was a savoury pie made with a combination of ingredients, a 'medley' of left-over cooked meats. This is a Derbyshire recipe for medley pie, where it is flavoured with sage and onions.

> 225g/8oz shortcrust pastry
> 225g/8oz lean bacon rashers, de-rinded
> 350g/12oz left-over pieces of cooked meat, such as beef,
>   lamb, rabbit, chicken, pork
> 1 onion
> 1 dessertspoonful finely chopped fresh sage leaves
>   (or one teaspoonful dried chopped sage)
> 1 egg, beaten
> Salt and pepper to taste
> 300ml/ ½ pint brown stock
> A little fat or oil for frying

Pre-heat the oven to 190°C/375°F/Gas Mark 5.

Cut the bacon into pieces, and peel and chop the onion. Heat a little fat or oil in a pan, and fry the onion with the bacon until soft, then put into an ovenproof pie dish together with the meat that is being used. Sprinkle over the sage and seasoning to taste, and pour over the stock.

Roll out the pastry on a floured surface. Place the pastry over the pie, seal to the rim of the pie dish and trim the edges. Make a slit in the centre of the pastry lid to allow steam to escape. Brush the pastry with the beaten egg to glaze, then bake in the pre-heated oven for about 1 hour, until the pastry is crisp and golden brown.

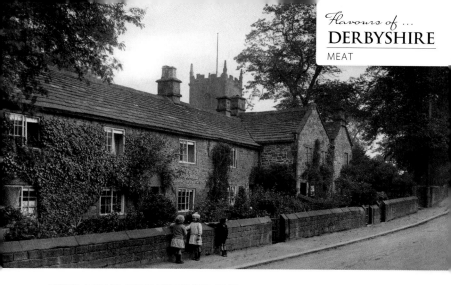

EYAM, THE PLAGUE COTTAGES 1910 69211

The Derbyshire village of Eyam is famous for the sacrifice made by its inhabitants during an outbreak of bubonic plague in 1665-66. The plague came to Eyam in a parcel of cloth sent to a tailor living in one of these cottages from plague-ravaged London; the cloth was infested with fleas carrying the deadly disease. Under the encouragement of their vicar, the villagers decided to put themselves into voluntarily quarantine and isolate Eyam from the outside world to contain the outbreak and prevent it spreading further afield. By the time the outbreak abated at least 257 villagers had died, but their brave stand undoubtedly saved the lives of thousands of people. During the period of isolation, food and medical supplies for the villagers were left on the outskirts of the village at either the Boundary Stone (beside a footpath leading out of the village towards Stoney Middleton) or Mompesson's Well (beside a minor road to the north of Eyam). The villagers left coins for payment, either cleansed in the bubbling water from the well spring or left in holes in the Boundary Stone filled with vinegar, to prevent infection spreading to those who were helping them.

Derbyshire's lush pastures and rich agricultural land along its river valleys provide succulent grazing for dairy cows, and meant that the county developed a strong cheesemaking tradition in the past, producing a number of local cheeses. Cheese would have been made in many farmhouses at one time and sold in the local markets, and there were also annual cheese fairs in Bakewell, Tideswell and Winster in the past, as well as weekly cheese markets at Derby, Chesterfield, Bakewell and Ashbourne.

Nowadays, the most famous cheeses from Derbyshire's cheesemaking heritage are probably Derby and Sage Derby.

Derby cheese has a smooth, mellow texture similar to Cheshire cheese, with a mild but distinctive flavour that improves significantly as the cheese matures. A variation of Derby cheese is Derby Sage, which has a green, marbled appearance and a fresh, herby flavour that is obtained by the inclusion of sage juice or finely chopped fresh sage leaves to the curds before the cheese is milled; sometimes the juice of nettles, spinach or parsley can also be used. In former years Sage Derby was a special celebratory cheese that was made to be eaten at country festivals between harvest time in the late summer until New Year's Eve, but nowadays it is made all year round. A particularly colourful variation of Sage Derby known as 'Chequerboard Derby' was often made at Christmas time in the past, when squares of sage-green cheese were alternated with golden squares that had been coloured with marigold juice. The custom of adding sage during the manufacturing process began in the 17th century, when the herb was believed to be beneficial to health and was put in the cheese for its medicinal properties.

Even though Sage Derby is one of England's oldest and most famous cheeses, only a few companies in the country make it nowadays. A very good Sage Derby cheese is produced by Fowlers of Earlswood, near Solihull, a family company that moved there from Derbyshire in 1918. Both Derby cheese and Sage Derby cheese can be hard to find nowadays, but are well worth seeking out from specialist cheese shops and online suppliers.

Flavours of ...
DERBYSHIRE
CHEESE & VEGETABLES

CHATSWORTH HOUSE 1886 18644

RECIPE

SAGE DERBY SOUFFLÉES

Sage Derby cheese makes a particularly good soufflé. The sage in the cheese adds an extra dimension to the flavour of the dish, and also gives it an unusual colour. This recipe is for small, individual soufflées. They make an ideal starter dish, perhaps served with brown bread and butter. They should be served as soon as they are cooked, so make sure your diners are ready and waiting at the table! If you can't find Sage Derby, use an alternative tasty cheese of choice, such as Cheddar or Stilton – another cheese which has Derbyshire connections (see page 16). Serves 6.

> 50g/2oz butter
> 50g/2oz plain flour
> 200ml/7fl oz milk
> 75g/3oz Sage Derby cheese, finely grated
> Salt and pepper
> 2 eggs, separated

Pre-heat the oven to 190°C/375°F/Gas Mark 5. Grease 6 individual ramekin dishes and place them on a baking tray.

Put the butter, flour and milk in a saucepan. Heat, whisking continuously, until the butter has melted and the sauce has thickened, boiled and become smooth. Reduce the heat to low and simmer gently for 2 minutes, stirring. Remove the pan from the heat and add the cheese, stirring it into the sauce until it has melted. Season to taste with salt and pepper. Beat in the 2 egg yolks. Whisk the 2 egg whites in a bowl until they are stiff and form peaks. Use a large metal spoon to fold the egg whites into the sauce, carefully but thoroughly. Divide the mixture between the 6 ramekin dishes, then place them on the baking tray in the pre-heated oven and bake for 30 minutes, until the soufflées are risen and golden brown. Serve immediately.

RECIPE

SAGE DERBY CHEESE AND POTATO CAKES

This is another recipe using colourful Sage Derby cheese, this time to make tasty potato cakes for a snack or a vegetable accompaniment to a meal. (Use an alternative hard, herb-flavoured cheese of choice if you can't find Sage Derby.) Potatoes first arrived in Britain from the New World in the late 16th century. Potato cultivation took a while to get established in Derbyshire, but eventually became widespread. In 'The History of the County of Derbyshire', published in 1829, Stephen Glover wrote of potato production in the county: 'This excellent root (solanus tuberosum) is widely and carefully cultivated in Derbyshire. It is said to have been first grown in the county at Baslow, so late as 1768, but since that period ample quantities have been raised here not only as human food but also for the support of cattle. Darley Dale is remarkable for the fine crop of potatoes produced there, and those produced in the neighbourhood of Ashover and Windley are much esteemed.'

> 450g/1 lb potatoes, peeled and cut into halves
> 25g/1oz butter or margarine
> 175g/6oz Sage Derby cheese (or alternative), finely grated
> Salt and pepper
> 1 egg, beaten
> A little plain flour
> Oil or dripping, for frying

Cook the potatoes in boiling salted water for 10-15 minutes until they are just tender. Drain the potatoes, then mash them with the butter or margarine. Add the grated cheese, beaten egg and salt and pepper to taste, and combine the mixture well. Flour your hands and form the mixture into about 8 small cakes. Flatten them slightly, and dredge both sides lightly with flour. Heat the fat or oil in a frying pan and fry the potato cakes in batches on a gentle heat for 1-2 minutes on each side, until they are golden brown. Alternatively, the potato cakes can be cooked on a greased baking tray in the oven, for about 15 minutes at 200°C/400°F/Gas Mark 6.

Derbyshire is one of the three designated counties in the country where Stilton cheese is legally allowed to be made. Stilton cheese was first developed in the villages on the borders of Leicestershire and Rutland, possibly as early as the 14th century. The cheese became famous in the 18th century when a dairywoman who lived near Melton Mowbray entered into a business arrangement with the landlord of the Bell Inn at Stilton (then in Huntingdonshire but now in Cambridgeshire) to market her cheese. The Bell Inn was a busy coaching inn and staging post along what is now the A1 between London and York, and the cheese became so popular with travellers staying at the inn that it took its name from the town where it was sold and distributed from, rather than where it was made. By the end of the 18th century Stilton cheese was being made in great quantities around Melton Mowbray, and by the early 20th century the making of Stilton cheese had extended to the neighbouring areas of Nottinghamshire and south Derbyshire to as far as Hartington. The Stilton cheese-makers then defined their product and sought legal protection for it to prevent the development of inferior imitation cheese. Stilton is one of the few cheeses granted a 'Protected Designation of Origin' status by the European Commission, which in 1969 ruled that 'Stilton is blue or white cheese made from full cream milk ...coming from English dairy herds in the district of Melton Mowbray and the surrounding areas falling within the counties of Leicestershire (now including Rutland), Derbyshire and Nottinghamshire'. There are strict codes for the quality of the cheese, and it can only be made in these designated counties.

The Hartington Creamery in Derbyshire was originally established by the Duke of Devonshire to produce the white, crumbly Derbyshire cheese. In 1900 it was taken over by Thomas Nuttall, a prize-winning Stilton cheese-maker from Melton Mowbray, who began producing Stilton at Hartington. Fine Stilton cheese continued to be made there for over 100 years, but sadly the Hartington Creamery closed down in 2009 and Stilton cheese is not currently being made anywhere in Derbyshire.

The Hartington Creamery was also famous for making Dovedale Blue, a soft, mild blue cheese with a creamy texture named after the valley of the River Dove beside which Hartington is located. This cheese was lost when the Hartington Creamery closed down, but has now been revived by the Staffordshire Cheese Company near Leek, just over the county border. The original Dovedale Blue cheese was granted Protected Designation of Origin (PDO) status by the EU, meaning it had to be made in a certain area and in a certain way. The revived cheese is made in the same way as the original version using milk from Derbyshire dairy herds, and as the Staffordshire Cheese Company makes the cheese within a 21 mile radius of the River Dove, it meets the legal criteria to still be called 'Dovedale Blue'. Despite the closure of its famous cheese factory, Hartington retains a cheese connection with the excellent Old Cheese Shop in its Market Place. If you can't get there yourself, the shop sells a wide variety of cheeses on its website: www.hartingtoncheeseshop.co.uk. The selection includes Derby, Sage Derby and, of course, Dovedale Blue.

DOVEDALE, THE ENTRANCE 1894 34264

RECIPE

DOVEDALE BLUE CHEESE AND BROCCOLI FLAN

This recipe uses Dovedale Blue cheese to make a savoury flan to serve either warm or cold for summer lunches, or taken on a picnic to eat cold. If you can't get Dovedale Blue, try making this with an alternative creamy blue cheese like St Agur, which is easily available in supermarkets. Alternatively, this recipe also works well with Stilton cheese.

> 175g/6oz plain flour
> 75g/3oz butter or margarine
> 225g/8oz trimmed weight of broccoli florets
> 175g/6oz Dovedale Blue cheese (or alternative – see above),
>   de-rinded and cut into small pieces
> 3 eggs, beaten
> 300ml/ ½ pint single cream
> Salt and freshly ground black pepper

Grease a flan tin about 25cms (10 inches) in diameter. Put the flour into a mixing bowl with a pinch of salt, and rub in the butter or margarine until the mixture resembles fine breadcrumbs. Add 2-3 tablespoonfuls of cold water, just enough to mix it together to form a firm dough, then knead the dough lightly until it is smooth and elastic. Roll out the dough on a lightly floured surface and use it to line the flan tin. Put the lined pastry case in the fridge to chill for 15 minutes. Pre-heat the oven to 190°C/375°F/Gas Mark 5.

Prick the pastry base all over with a fork, to allow air bubbles to escape during cooking. Line the pastry case with a piece of greaseproof paper and fill it with baking beans (or alternative, such as uncooked rice). Place the flan tin in the oven and bake blind for 10-15 minutes, until the pastry is just firm and lightly golden. Remove the tin from the oven, take out the baking beans and paper and return the tin to the oven for a further 5-7 minutes to dry out the pastry base. Remove the flan tin from the oven, reduce the oven temperature to 180°C/350°F/Gas Mark 4, and place a baking tray in the oven to heat up.

While the pastry case is cooking, prepare the broccoli florets. Bring a pan of water to the boil, and add the trimmed florets. Bring the water back to the boil, cook for 2 minutes, then remove from the heat and drain the broccoli thoroughly. Arrange the broccoli florets in the pastry case, and scatter the pieces of cheese over and around them.

Lightly beat or whisk together the beaten eggs and cream, and season to taste with salt and plenty of pepper (go easy on the salt if you are using Stilton as an alternative cheese, as this will already be quite salty). Pour the mixture into the pastry case over the broccoli and cheese. Place the flan tin on the baking tray in the oven and bake at the reduced temperature for 30-40 minutes, until the filling is risen and just firm to the touch.

This should not be eaten hot, straight from the oven, but leave it to cool a little and eat it warm, or otherwise leave it to cool completely before eating. Either way, it is best eaten the same day as it is cooked.

CHESTERFIELD, STEPHENSON PLACE 1914 67563

RECIPE

DERBYSHIRE STUFFED ONIONS

By the late 12th century Chesterfield had become the major market town of north-east Derbyshire. In his charter of 1204, King John granted a weekly market at Chesterfield on Saturdays, and a fair at the festival of the Holy Rood in September. The market at Chesterfield was for corn (particularly wheat and oats), and all kinds of provisions. A later charter of 1631 granted four fairs a year, in February, May, July and September. The September fair lasted for eight days, and was particularly known for produce such as cheese, apples and onions.

    4 large onions
    50g/2oz fresh breadcrumbs
    50g/2oz bacon, finely chopped
    1 teaspoonful of sage, finely chopped
    Salt and pepper to taste
    25g/1oz butter
    25g/1oz grated cheese
    A little chopped fresh parsley to garnish

Remove the onion skins, but keep the onions whole. Place the onions in a large pan of boiling water, and boil for 20 minutes until they are softened.

Pre-heat the oven to 200°C/400°F/Gas Mark 6.

Remove the onions from the pan and drain, then leave to cool for a few minutes. Cut the top off each onion, then scoop out the centre and finely chop. Mix together the chopped cooked onions, breadcrumbs, bacon and sage, and season to taste, then mix in the butter well. Use the mixture to fill each onion shell, and sprinkle the tops with the grated cheese. Stand the onions on a baking tray, and bake in the pre-heated oven for about 30 minutes. Serve garnished with the chopped parsley.

Chesterfield is famous for the twisting spire of the parish church of St Mary and All Saints. The lead-covered timber spire is 70m (228ft) high, and leans out of true some 1.83m (6ft) to the south and over 1.2m (4ft) to the west. The famous twisting spire is still moving! Although the spire looks as if it will collapse at any second, it has a very low centre of gravity and is therefore quite safe. The twisting is thought to have been caused by the heat of the sun on the lead plates of the roof, which in turn warped the unseasoned timber that had been used in the spire's construction at the end of the 13th century. However, there are a number of traditional folklore explanations about how Chesterfield's parish church came by its famous twisted spire. One says that a magician managed to persuade a blacksmith in Bolsover to shoe the Devil's cloven hooves. After he drove the first nail into the Devil's foot, the Devil howled in pain and took flight, and lashed out in agony as he flew over Chesterfield, catching the spire with his foot and causing it to twist round. Another version says that the tower buckled under the Devil's weight when he sat on it. There are also two other Derbyshire interpretations for the twist, neither of which is very complimentary to Chesterfield's inhabitants! One tells how the Devil visited Chesterfield one day and sat on the top of the church spire so that he could have a good look at the place. As it was windy, the Devil twisted his tail around the spire to prevent himself from falling. When he heard a local person speaking the truth about something, he was so surprised and shocked at this uncommon event in the town that he flew off in a hurry without unwinding his tail, causing the spire to twist. The other story tells how the spire itself was so amazed to hear that a local girl getting married in the church was still a virgin that it twisted round in an effort to see this wonder for itself. According to this tale, the spire will straighten itself up again should such a rare event ever occur again!

CHESTERFIELD, ST MARY AND
ALL SAINTS' PARISH CHURCH
1902 48888

Buxton's warm springs are thought to have been discovered by the Romans, and by Tudor times their efficacious effects and mineralised water led to the development of Buxton as a spa town. The area of lower Buxton around the baths was developed through the 17th and 18th centuries by successive Dukes of Devonshire (of Chatsworth House, to the east of Buxton, and the principal landowners of the area), culminating in the impressive investment of the 5th Duke, who commissioned the Crescent and stables, the Square, Hall Bank and St John's Church, all between 1780 and 1811. The Georgian spa of Buxton enjoyed modest success, but the most spectacular growth of the town came in the sixty years from 1850, when the 7th Duke of Devonshire invested much of the money he gained from his mineral interests in the Peak District towards expanding Buxton into one of the most popular and fashionable spa towns in England. The town became a busy and prosperous centre for water medicine and hydrotherapy, and a very smart inland resort.

BUXTON, THE CRESCENT 1886 I8649

SUMMER PUDDING

In the mid 19th century the development of treatment programmes using immersion in cold water, combined with exercise and carefully regulated dietary regimes, gave rise to the hydropathic movement, and hydrotherapy treatments became very popular in Derbyshire's spa towns like Buxton, Matlock and Matlock Bath. Summer Pudding was a popular dessert with visitors to hydropathic establishments in spa towns because it was lighter than pastry-based puddings, which were thought to be heavy and indigestible. For this reason it was sometimes known as Hydropathic Pudding.

> 10 slices of crustless white bread – use bread from a proper loaf, not a sliced and wrapped one, for best results
> 3 tablespoonfuls of milk
> 675g/1½ lbs soft fruit – use a variety of fruits such as raspberries, cherries, redcurrants, blackcurrants, white currants, loganberries or (sparingly) strawberries
> 115g/4oz caster sugar

Reserve a few pieces of fresh fruit to decorate. Lightly butter a pudding basin of 1 litre/1¾ pint capacity. Moisten the bread with milk. Hull, stone or top and tail the fruit as necessary. Cook it all very gently in a saucepan in the sugar for 4-5 minutes until the sugar melts and the juices run. Spoon off a few spoonfuls of the juice as it cools and reserve. Line the sides and bottom of the pudding basin with the bread slices, cutting them to fit where necessary and checking that there are no spaces between them. Reserve enough bread slices for a lid. Pour in the fruit, which should come almost to the top, and cover closely with the remaining bread. Put a small plate over the top (it should just fit inside the rim of the basin), and weight it with something heavy. Leave to press overnight in the fridge.

To serve, remove the weight and the plate. Place a deep serving dish over the top of the pudding basin and reverse quickly so that the pudding comes out easily in one piece. Pour the remaining juices slowly all over the pudding, especially over the places where the juice has not seeped through the bread slices thoroughly. Keep cold until ready to serve, then decorate with a few pieces of fruit and serve with cream.

RECIPE

DERBYSHIRE GOOSEBERRY PUDDING

In many parts of England in the past, including Derbyshire, a gooseberry pudding or pie was the traditional fare for Whit Sunday (50 days after Easter) at the end of May. This is the day on which the Christian Church celebrates Pentecost, and is also the time of year when gooseberries first come into season. Gooseberries are also known as 'Feeberries' in some parts of Derbyshire. This is a version of the batter puddings for which Derbyshire is famous. Other fruits can also be used if preferred, such as blackberries or apples, peeled and cored and cut into small pieces.

> 175g/6oz plain flour
> A pinch of salt
> ½ teaspoonful baking powder
> 2 eggs
> 350ml/12 fl oz milk
> 450g/1 lb gooseberries
> 75g/3oz caster sugar
> A small amount of fat or oil for cooking

Sieve the flour into a bowl with the salt and baking powder. Form a well in the centre and add the eggs, and beat them into the flour. Gradually add the milk, beating the mixture until it has formed a smooth batter. Cover the basin with a cloth and leave to stand.

Pre-heat the oven to 190°C/375°F/Gas Mark 5. Wash, top and tail the gooseberries. Place a little fat or oil in an oven tin, and put in the oven to heat up. When the fat or oil is hot, pour the batter into the tin, add the prepared gooseberries and sprinkle with the sugar. Bake in the oven for about 1 hour, then serve with extra sugar to taste if necessary.

GOYT VALLEY, STEPPING STONES 1914 67587

RECIPE

BILBERRY AND APPLE PIE

In late summer and early autumn the high ground of the Peak District is abundant with wild bilberries, especially around the Ladybower Reservoir in the Upper Derwent Valley. In Derbyshire, bilberries are also known as windberries. They grow on small low-lying bushes with dark green leaves and are hard work to pick, but well worth the effort. They have a delicious flavour and are excellent for cooking, as well as being good eaten raw. For centuries local people have gathered them to make into delicious pies, puddings and other delicacies, as well as for making dye and using them for medicinal purposes. A recipe for a Bilberry and Apple Pie is given here. Traditionally, a Bilberry Pie includes a small amount of finely chopped fresh mint, which highlights the delicate flavour of the berries and gives the pie a delicious fresh taste. If you can't get out to pick your own bilberries, you can use commercially grown blueberries in this pie instead.

<u>For the sweet shortcrust pastry:</u>
350g/12oz plain flour
A pinch of salt
75g/3oz butter, cut into small pieces
75g/3oz lard or pastry margarine, cut into small pieces
50g/2oz caster sugar, plus one extra tablespoonful of caster sugar to glaze the pastry
1 egg, separated
2-3 tablespoons cold water or milk

<u>For the fruit filling:</u>
450g/1 lb bilberries (or blueberries, as an alternative)
2 cooking apples
150g/5oz caster sugar
1 teaspoonful finely chopped fresh mint leaves

To make the pastry, sift the flour and salt into a bowl. Rub the fat into the flour with your fingertips until the mixture resembles breadcrumbs. Stir in the sugar, the egg yolk and enough cold water or milk to form a smooth dough. Wrap in cling film and leave in the fridge to chill and rest for 30 minutes before using.

Pre-heat the oven to 200°C/400°F/Gas Mark 6. Remove the cores from the apples with an apple corer, but do not peel them. Stand the apples in an ovenproof dish, add 2 tablespoonfuls of water to the dish and bake in the pre-heated oven for 40-45 minutes, until the apples are tender. When cooked, remove from the oven (but leave the oven on at the same temperature), scrape out the pulp from the apples and mix it with the bilberries, sugar and chopped mint.

Place a baking tray in the oven to heat up. Grease a deep pie dish or tin, 20-24cms (8-9 ins) in diameter. Roll out two-thirds of the pastry on a lightly floured surface and use it to line the pie dish. Turn out the fruit mixture into the pie dish and spread it evenly over the pastry base. Roll out the remaining pastry to form a lid, moisten the top edge of the pastry base with a little water or milk, and place the pastry lid over the filling. Press down on the pastry edges all round the pie, making sure that they are firmly sealed together, then trim off any excess pastry. Cut two short slits in the centre of the lid to allow steam to escape during cooking. Brush the top of the pie with the egg white beaten with the extra tablespoonful of caster sugar. Place the pie dish on the hot baking tray in the oven (this helps the pastry base to cook through) and bake at 200°C/400°F/Gas Mark 6 for ten minutes, then reduce the temperature to 180°C/350°F/Gas Mark 4 and cook for a further 30 minutes until the pastry is crisp and golden. Serve either warm or cold, but not hot straight from the oven.

RECIPE

BLACKBERRY PUDDING

Wild blackberries also grow in profusion in many parts of Derbyshire. They are ripe from early August until late September. Wild blackberries in season have a much better flavour than the commercially grown blackberries that are available in supermarkets all year round nowadays – and it's fun to go out in the countryside foraging for them. This makes a delicious pudding with blackberries beneath a sponge topping. Serves 4, so increase the quantities to make a larger pudding.

<u>For the filling:</u>
450g/1 lb blackberries
115g/4oz caster sugar
1 tablespoonful plain flour
A small pinch of ground cinnamon

<u>For the topping:</u>
50g/2oz butter or margarine, softened to room temperature
50g/2oz caster sugar
1 egg
115g/4oz self-raising flour
A small pinch of salt
2 tablespoonfuls milk
Grated zest of one lemon
One extra dessertspoonful of caster sugar, to finish

Pre-heat the oven to 180C/350°F/Gas Mark 4 and butter a 1.2 litre (2 pint) ovenproof pie or pudding dish.

To prepare the fruit filling, place the blackberries, caster sugar, flour and cinnamon in a large mixing bowl. Stir gently to coat the blackberries and mix it all together, then transfer all the mixture to the prepared baking dish.

To make the topping, beat the butter or margarine and sugar together until the mixture is light and fluffy. Beat the egg and gradually mix it in, a little at a time, then beat in the flour, salt, milk and lemon zest. Spread the mixture smoothly over the fruit, and sprinkle the extra sugar over the surface. Bake in the pre-heated oven for about 30 minutes, until the sponge topping is risen and golden brown, and firm to the touch. Serve with cream or custard.

HATHERSAGE, DOWN THE VALE 1932 85243

BAKEWELL, THE RUTLAND ARMS HOTEL, RUTLAND SQUARE 1914
67616

One of Derbyshire's food legends is the delicious Bakewell Pudding, which according to local lore was created by mistake in the 19th century by an inexperienced cook at what is now the Rutland Arms Hotel in Bakewell (then known as the White Horse Inn). There are several versions of the story, but one is that she misunderstood the instructions of her mistress, Mrs Greaves, about making a strawberry tart for guests at the inn. Instead of adding butter, eggs and sugar to the pastry to enrich it and then spreading strawberry jam on top, the flustered cook lined the dish with pastry, put in the jam and then spread the egg mixture on top. Despite the error, the resulting product was well-received by the inn's guests, and the Bakewell Pudding became a popular local dish. Whatever the truth of its origins, a Bakewell Pudding is a wonderful thing, and deserves to be much more popular outside Bakewell itself than it is.

BAKEWELL PUDDING

A Bakewell Pudding is made with puff pastry spread with strawberry or raspberry jam, and filled with a sweet, buttery, egg-custard-like filling. It is far removed from the better-known Bakewell Tart, which resembles a frangipane tart with a more solid filling of almond sponge encased in shortcrust pastry, spread with raspberry or apricot jam. The use of puff pastry results in the pastry edge curving inwards as the filling cooks, giving the Bakewell Pudding its distinctive floppy-edged shape. It may not look elegant, but it is delicious. According to the earliest versions of the recipe for Bakewell Pudding, ground almonds should not be included. However, they are now so closely identified with this dish, and its near relative the Bakewell Tart, that they are included here as an optional ingredient. There is also a similar Derbyshire dish to this called Buxton Pudding, where breadcrumbs are used instead of the ground almonds.

175g/6oz puff pastry
75g/3oz butter, softened
75g/3oz caster sugar
3 eggs, beaten
A quarter of a teaspoonful almond essence (optional)
1 tablespoonful ground almonds (optional)
2 tablespoonfuls strawberry jam

Pre-heat the oven to 190°C/375°F/Gas Mark 5 and place a baking tray in the oven to heat up. Grease a large oval pie dish or a pie or flan tin 20-24cms (8-9 inches) in diameter. Roll out the pastry on a lightly floured surface and use it to line the pie dish or tin. Spread the jam evenly over the pastry base. Beat together the softened butter and sugar until it is light and fluffy. Gradually beat in the beaten eggs, a little at a time, alternating with the ground almonds. Add the almond essence and beat well. Pour the egg mixture into the pastry case, spreading it evenly right to the edges so that all the jam is covered. Place the pie dish or tin on the baking sheet in the pre-heated oven (this helps the pastry base to cook through). Bake for 25-30 minutes, until the filling is risen and just firm to the touch. Remove from the oven and leave for a few minutes for the filling to set before eating hot, or leave to cool completely and eat cold. Serve with cream or ice-cream.

WHEN THE
PANCAKE BELL RINGS ...

The 40 day period leading up to the Christian religious festival of Easter in the spring is known as Lent, which begins on Ash Wednesday. Shrove Tuesday is the day before Ash Wednesday and was traditionally the day for 'shriving' – confessing sins and asking forgiveness – before Lent began. Lent was a period of religious fasting and dietary austerity in the past, when eggs, butter, meat and certain other foods were not allowed to be eaten. This is the origin of what we now call Pancake Day, when making pancakes on Shrove Tuesday was a way of using up some 'forbidden foods' in the larder before Lent began. The bell that was rung in parish churches on Shrove Tuesday morning in the past, calling people to church to be shriven, was often called the 'Pancake Bell'.

Shrove Tuesday was traditionally a day for fun, feasting and pranks, the last chance for merrymaking or wild behaviour before the rigours of Lent. In Derby, the ringing of the 'Pancake Bell' on Shrove Tuesday in the past was the signal for wild football matches to be played through the town between teams from rivalling parishes – this is the origin of the phrase 'a Derby game', when two sporting sides from the same town or city play each other. Derby's Shrovetide football matches were riotous affairs involving a large number of townspeople, although in theory they were played between the parishioners of St Peter's Church, at the junction of East Street, St Peter's Street and St Peter's Churchyard, and All Saints' Church at Iron Gate (which was granted cathedral status in 1927 and is now Derby Cathedral, the smallest Anglican cathedral in England). When the 'Pancake Bell' was rung, the players descended upon the Market Place, where the ball was thrown up and mayhem ensued. Rules were few and far between, and the playing area was the streets of the town. On Ash Wednesday the game was repeated, but this time restricted to those considered too young to play on Shrove Tuesday.

**DERBY, IRON GATE AND ALL SAINTS' CHURCH
(NOW DERBY CATHEDRAL) 1896** 37780

The following rhyme describes the bells of the churches around Derby, and was traditionally chanted at the beginning of the Shrovetide football match:

> *Pancakes and fritters,*
> *Say All Saints and St Peter's;*
> *When will the ball come?*
> *Say the bells of St Alkmund's;*
> *At two they will throw,*
> *Says St Werabo;*
> *Oh! Very well,*
> *Says little St Michael!*

Derby's Shrovetide football matches were disliked by many townsfolk because they caused damage to property and disruption to trade, and they were finally banned in 1860. However, a similar custom still takes place through the streets of Ashbourne in Derbyshire on Shrove Tuesday, where the Royal Shrovetide Football attracts hundreds of contestants.

DERBY, THE CORNMARKET 1896 37779

RECIPE

DERBY CAKES

Derby began to develop into an industrial town after Thomas and John Lombe established Derby's silk mill around 1718. The famous Derby porcelain factory was established in the 1750s and an iron-founding industry followed, helped by local supplies of coal. The building of the Derby Canal in 1796 proved to be a key element in turning a prosperous market town into a centre of industry. Derby's modern growth was due to it being chosen as the headquarters and main workshops for the Midland Railway, and good railway connections led to other industries opening for business. A major employer in 20th-century Derby was Rolls-Royce, referred to locally as 'the Royce'; cars were made there until 1946, but aero engine production then took over. Derby has subsequently become one of the major industrial and engineering centres of the Midlands. Situated on the edge of the Peak District National Park, Derby is a now a vibrant modern city, but still retains much of its Georgian architectural heritage.

> 450g/1 lb plain flour
> 225g/8oz butter or margarine
> 225g/8oz brown sugar
> 225g/8oz currants
> A good pinch of ground cinnamon, to taste
> 1 egg, beaten
> A little milk for mixing

Pre-heat the oven to 190°C/375°F/Gas Mark 5 and grease a baking tray. Rub the butter or margarine into the flour until the mixture resembles fine breadcrumbs. Add the sugar, currants and cinnamon, and mix the ingredients well together. Add the egg, and enough milk to form a stiff dough. Knead the dough until it is smooth and pliable. Roll out the dough on a lightly floured surface to about 5mm (¼ inch) thick. Cut the dough into small rounds, and place them on the greased baking tray. Bake in the pre-heated oven for 10-15 minutes, until they are golden brown.

RECIPE

DERBYSHIRE LEMON RICE TARTS

These delicious little tarts have a lemon-flavoured sponge filling made with ground rice – you will find this next to the pudding rice on supermarket shelves. This amount should make 12 tarts.

>225g/8oz shortcrust pastry
>50g/2oz butter
>50g/2oz ground rice
>¼ teaspoonful baking powder
>115g/4oz caster sugar
>50g/2oz currants
>1 egg, beaten
>Grated zest and juice of 1 large lemon

Pre-heat the oven to180°C/350°F/Gas Mark 4. Grease 12 patty tins. Roll out the pastry and cut it into enough rounds to line the patty tins.

Melt the butter in a saucepan over a gentle heat, then put to one side and allow to cool for a few minutes.

Put the ground rice into a mixing bow. Add the baking powder and mix well, then add the sugar and currants. Pour in the melted butter and mix it in, then stir in the beaten egg. Add the lemon zest and juice and combine it all well together. Half fill each pastry-lined patty tin with the mixture.

Bake in the pre-heated oven for 20-25 minutes, until the filling is risen and golden brown and is firm to the touch. Remove from the oven and leave to cool in the tins for five minutes then turn out the tarts onto a wire tray and leave to cool completely.

**ASHBOURNE, THE GREEN MAN AND BLACK'S HEAD ROYAL HOTEL
1886** 18577

Like many Midlands counties, Derbyshire has its own versions of
gingerbread, and that from Ashbourne is particularly famous. A
local tradition says that the recipe was brought to Ashbourne by
a French prisoner of war who was billeted in the town during the
Napoleonic Wars of the early 19th century. He made the gingerbread
in Ashbourne in 1805 and his recipe was copied and widely used in
the town; it proved popular, and Ashbourne soon became famous
for its local delicacy. Ashbourne Gingerbread is still made and sold
in the town by the Spencers bakery in the market place. The exact
recipe is a trade secret, and the recipe on the opposite page is an
approximation.

RECIPE

ASHBOURNE GINGERBREAD BISCUITS

Ashbourne Gingerbread is rather similar to shortbread, with a crisp, biscuit texture. It is pale in colour, with a sweet, mild ginger flavour enhanced by the lemon peel. A pretty crinkled pattern forms on the top of these gingerbread biscuits as they cook. This amount should make 8-10 biscuits.

> 175g/6oz butter or margarine
> 115g/4oz caster sugar
> 225g/8oz self-raising flour
> 2 level teaspoonfuls ground ginger
> A pinch of salt
> Finely grated rind of 1 lemon
> 25g/1oz candied lemon peel if possible,
>   otherwise mixed peel, finely chopped (optional)

Pre-heat the oven to 180°C/350°F/Gas Mark 4.

Cream together the butter or margarine and sugar until it is fluffy. Sift in the flour, ginger and salt, and add the lemon peel, and the candied peel if used. Knead the mixture to form a smooth dough. Form the dough into a large sausage shape, then cut across it to make round slices about 4cm (1½ inches) thick. Place the slices on a greased baking tin, spaced apart to leave room for expansion during cooking. Bake in the pre-heated oven for about 15-20 minutes, until they are risen and golden but not too browned – the gingerbreads should remain quite pale. Allow the gingerbreads to cool slightly before removing them from the tin, then leave on a wire rack to cool completely. Store in an airtight tin.

**MATLOCK BATH, SOUTH PROMENADE AND
HEIGHTS OF ABRAHAM c1877** M47502

BONSALL, THE PIG OF LEAD INN 1892 31300

The mineral resources of the Derwent gorge have been exploited by generations of miners and quarrymen since at least Roman times. At one time, Derbyshire was one of the main centres for lead mining – around 100,000 mine shafts have been located and recorded – and there are many reminders hereabouts of 't'owd man', as the old lead miners were called. Information about the mining heritage of the area can be found in the mining museum run by the Peak District Mines Historical Society in Matlock Bath, which also features simulated mine shafts and passages for the visitor to explore. On the right hand side of this 1890s' view is the Pig of Lead Inn at Bonsall, a village sheltered in a nook of the limestone hills to the west of Matlock Bath which was once an important centre of the lead mining industry of the White Peak. The name of the pub recalls the industry – a 'pig' was the name for a lead ingot. The inn closed some years ago and the building is now run as a Bed & Breakfast establishment, but is still known as the Pig of Lead.

RECIPE

DERBYSHIRE OATCAKES

Oatcakes as well as bread were basic daily fare in the Peak District of Derbyshire in the past, where oatmeal formed the mainstay of many people's diet in the 18th and 19th centuries. In 1813 Sir Humphrey Davy recorded: 'The Derbyshire miners in winter prefer oatcakes to wheaten bread ... such nourishment enables them to support their strength and perform their labours better.' Derbyshire Oatcakes are similar to pancakes but are made with oatmeal, and are served rolled up and filled with either sweet or savoury fillings. Try them with ham, bacon, mushrooms, grated cheese, egg, and sausage, or for a quick snack wrapped around cheese and warmed in a microwave or under a grill, or eat them whilst still warm from the pan, spread with honey, jam or golden syrup. This recipe makes about four Derbyshire oatcakes, which are smaller and thicker than the better-known Staffordshire variety – increase the quantity of milk and water to 900ml/1½ pints to make a larger quantity of thinner oatcakes, if preferred.

> 225g/8oz fine oatmeal
> 225g/8oz plain flour
> 1 teaspoonful salt
> 15g/½ oz fresh yeast, or 1½ teaspoonfuls quick-acting dried yeast
> 600ml/1 pint warm milk and water, mixed half and half
> 1 teaspoonful sugar

Add the salt to the flour and oatmeal. Dissolve the yeast with a little warm milk and water, add the sugar, then leave it until it becomes frothy. When the yeast mixture is ready, mix the dry ingredients with the yeast and the rest of the warm liquid to make a batter. Cover the mixture with a clean cloth and leave in a warm place for 1 hour.

To cook the oatcakes, use a well-greased griddle or heavy frying pan. Put enough batter on the hot griddle to make an oatcake of your own preferred size; cook, and turn after 2-3 minutes and cook for a further 2-3 minutes - both sides should be golden brown. Serve with the filling of your choice.

RECIPE

THOR CAKE

Thor Cake, also known as Tharf Cake, is a recipe from Derbyshire for a cake that was eaten on special occasions such as Bonfire Night (5th November) and Wakes Weeks, a time of celebrations and fairs held in various towns and villages throughout the county on different dates (see page 48). In some parts of the county, friends and families would get together on Bonfire Night for 'Thor (or Tharf) Cake Joinings' – they would all contribute money to make Thor Cakes, then meet up at one of their homes to make and eat the cakes together. There are several versions of Thor Cakes – the recipe given here is for one large loaf-like cake, but they are also made with the dough rolled out and either cut into thin rounds for baking as biscuits, or thicker rounds for baking as individual small round cakes.

> 225g/8oz oatmeal
> 225g/8oz self-raising flour
> 225g/8oz brown sugar
> Half a teaspoonful baking powder
> Half a teaspoonful ground ginger
> Half a teaspoonful salt
> Half a teaspoonful ground allspice
> 50g/2oz candied peel
> 225g/8oz butter
> 175g/6oz black treacle

Pre-heat the oven to 190°C/375°F/Gas Mark 5.

Add the baking powder to the flour and oatmeal in a mixing bowl, then mix in the sugar, ginger, salt, allspice and peel. Heat the butter and treacle together in a saucepan, and when it has all melted and blended together add the mixture to the mixing bowl and combine all the ingredients well together. Put the mixture into a well-greased loaf-style cake tin and bake in the pre-heated oven for about 45 minutes.

**ASHFORD-IN-THE-WATER
THE DAY'S WORK DONE
c1955** A324001

MELBOURNE WAKES CAKES

Wakes Weeks were a time of celebrations and fairs in many Derbyshire towns and villages in the past. Their dates would vary in different places, but they were usually held in the summer. In many places, Wakes Weeks also involved the delightful tradition of well dressing for which a number of towns and villages in the county are still famous. Well-dressing probably originated in pagan times as a form of thanksgiving around springs and wells for a water supply, but later became a Christian tradition. The local wells are 'dressed' with spectacular decorations in religious or biblical themes that are made by creating a large framework of wood into which clay is worked. Flowers, petals – in fact anything natural – is then used to create a picture. The photograph on the opposite page shows the 'dressed' Town Well at Tideswell in the Peak District being admired by a group of visitors. During Wakes Weeks, special cakes unique to the village would be eaten. There are a number of local recipes, but this one given comes from Melbourne, south of Derby. This amount makes about 10 cakes, which are actually more like biscuits.

> 225g/8oz plain flour
> Half a teaspoonful baking powder
> 115g/4oz butter or margarine, cut into small pieces
> 75g/3oz caster sugar
> 75g/3oz currants
> 1 egg
> 1 tablespoonful double cream

Pre-heat the oven to 190°C/375°F/Gas Mark 5 and grease a baking tray. Sieve the flour and baking powder together into a bowl. Rub in the butter or margarine until the mixture resembles breadcrumbs. Stir in the sugar and currants. Beat the egg with the cream, add it to the mixture and beat it together well so that it is all well combined into a stiff dough. Knead the dough lightly (sprinkle a little extra flour over it if necessary, if it is too sticky) then roll it out on a lightly floured surface to about 2cms (¾ inch) thick. Cut out rounds about 5cm (2 inches) in diameter. Place the rounds on the baking tray and bake in the pre-heated oven for about 15 minutes, until they are risen, golden and crisp, but not over-browned. Cool on a wire tray.

TIDESWELL, WELL DRESSING 2000 T46701

THOU CROWNEST THE YEAR WITH THY GOODNESS

THOU VISITEST THE EARTH AND WATEREST IT

RECIPE

DERBYSHIRE PARKIN

Parkin is a dark sweet cake made from oatmeal as well as flour that is a heavy, sticky cake due to the addition of black treacle. Parkin was traditionally eaten in many parts of the country in the past on Bonfire Night (or Guy Fawkes Night) on 5th November, but its older tradition is associated with the feast days marking the beginning of winter, around the time of Halloween on 1st October, All Saints' (or All Hallows') Day on 1st November and All Souls' Day on 2nd November.

> 450g/1 lb oatmeal
> 225g/8oz plain flour
> 115g/4oz butter or margarine
> 225g/8oz black treacle
> 225g/8oz golden syrup
> 50g/2oz soft brown sugar
> 75g/3oz candied peel and lemon rind
> ½ teaspoonful of baking powder
> A good pinch of ground allspice

Pre-heat the oven to 190°C/375°F/Gas Mark 5.

Mix together the oatmeal and flour, and rub in the butter or margarine. Add the treacle, golden syrup, sugar, candied peel, lemon rind, baking powder and allspice. Mix together, adding a little warmed water if necessary. Knead the mixture so that all the ingredients are well mixed in. Grease a deep baking tin, and pour in the mixture – the cooked parkin should be about 5cm (2 inches) thick. Place in the pre-heated oven and bake for 1-1½ hours. When cooked, cut the parkin into squares and leave in the tin to cool.

Store in an airtight container. Parkin is best left for several days before eating, to allow it to soften and become sticky.

RECIPE

DERBYSHIRE FRUIT LOAF

This recipe for a spiced fruit loaf flavoured with marmalade comes from the Peak District. It makes a delicious teabread to serve cut into slices at teatime. The marmalade helps to keep it moist as well as giving it a lovely flavour. You can use either fine cut or chunky cut marmalade – whichever is your own preference for spreading on your breakfast toast! When making this, remember to soak the dried fruit in (milkless) tea overnight before you need it – this makes the fruit lovely and juicy, resulting in a deliciously tasty tea bread.

450g/1 lb mixed dried fruit – currants, raisins, sultanas
225g/8oz sugar
300ml/½ pint hot (milk-less) tea
1 egg
450g/1 lb self-raising flour
Half a teaspoonful mixed spice
Half a teaspoonful ground nutmeg
2 tablespoonfuls marmalade

Put the dried fruit, sugar and hot tea in a bowl and leave to soak overnight.

Pre-heat the oven to 150°C/300°F/Gas Mark 2. Grease and line a 900g/2 lb loaf tin.

Stir the egg, flour, spices and marmalade into the fruit, sugar and remaining tea. Pour into the greased and lined loaf tin and bake in the pre-heated oven for 1½ - 2 hours until firm to the touch, or until a knife or skewer pushed into the cake comes out clean. When cooled, store in an airtight tin. Serve cut into slices, spread with butter.

**CHAPEL-EN-LE-FRITH, THE VIEW FROM ECCLES PIKE
c1940** C400021

FRANCIS FRITH

PIONEER VICTORIAN PHOTOGRAPHER

Francis Frith, founder of the world-famous photographic archive, was a complex and multi-talented man. A devout Quaker and a highly successful Victorian businessman, he was philosophical by nature and pioneering in outlook. By 1855 he had already established a wholesale grocery business in Liverpool, and sold it for the astonishing sum of £200,000, which is the equivalent today of over £15,000,000. Now in his thirties, and captivated by the new science of photography, Frith set out on a series of pioneering journeys up the Nile and to the Near East.

INTRIGUE AND EXPLORATION

He was the first photographer to venture beyond the sixth cataract of the Nile. Africa was still the mysterious 'Dark Continent', and Stanley and Livingstone's historic meeting was a decade into the future. The conditions for picture taking confound belief. He laboured for hours in his wicker dark-room in the sweltering heat of the desert, while the volatile chemicals fizzed dangerously in their trays. Back in London he exhibited his photographs and was 'rapturously cheered' by members of the Royal Society. His reputation as a photographer was made overnight.

VENTURE OF A LIFE-TIME

By the 1870s the railways had threaded their way across the country, and Bank Holidays and half-day Saturdays had been made obligatory by Act of Parliament. All of a sudden the working man and his family were able to enjoy days out, take holidays, and see a little more of the world.

With typical business acumen, Francis Frith foresaw that these new tourists would enjoy having souvenirs to commemorate their days out. For the next thirty years he travelled the country by train and by pony and trap, producing fine photographs of seaside resorts and beauty spots that were keenly bought by millions of Victorians. These prints were painstakingly pasted into family albums and pored over during the dark nights of winter, rekindling precious memories of summer excursions. Frith's studio was soon supplying retail shops all over the country, and by 1890 F Frith & Co had become the greatest specialist photographic publishing company in the world, with over 2,000 sales outlets, and pioneered the picture postcard.

FRANCIS FRITH'S LEGACY

Francis Frith had died in 1898 at his villa in Cannes, his great project still growing. By 1970 the archive he created contained over a third of a million pictures showing 7,000 British towns and villages.

Frith's legacy to us today is of immense significance and value, for the magnificent archive of evocative photographs he created provides a unique record of change in the cities, towns and villages throughout Britain over a century and more. Frith and his fellow studio photographers revisited locations many times down the years to update their views, compiling for us an enthralling and colourful pageant of British life and character.

We are fortunate that Frith was dedicated to recording the minutiae of everyday life. For it is this sheer wealth of visual data, the painstaking chronicle of changes in dress, transport, street layouts, buildings, housing and landscape that captivates us so much today, offering us a powerful link with the past and with the lives of our ancestors.

Computers have now made it possible for Frith's many thousands of images to be accessed almost instantly. The archive offers every one of us an opportunity to examine the places where we and our families have lived and worked down the years. Its images, depicting our shared past, are now bringing pleasure and enlightenment to millions around the world a century and more after his death.

For further information visit: www.francisfrith.com

INTERIOR DECORATION

Frith's photographs can be seen framed and as giant wall murals in thousands of pubs, restaurants, hotels, banks, retail stores and other public buildings throughout Britain. These provide interesting and attractive décor, generating strong local interest and acting as a powerful reminder of gentler days in our increasingly busy and frenetic world.

FRITH PRODUCTS

All Frith photographs are available as prints and posters in a variety of different sizes and styles. In the UK we also offer a range of other gift and stationery products illustrated with Frith photographs, although many of these are not available for delivery outside the UK – see our web site for more information on the products available for delivery in your country.

THE INTERNET

Over 100,000 photographs of Britain can be viewed and purchased on the Frith web site. The web site also includes memories and reminiscences contributed by our customers, who have personal knowledge of localities and of the people and properties depicted in Frith photographs. If you wish to learn more about a specific town or village you may find these reminiscences fascinating to browse. Why not add your own comments if you think they would be of interest to others? See **www.francisfrith.com**

PLEASE HELP US BRING FRITH'S PHOTOGRAPHS TO LIFE

Our authors do their best to recount the history of the places they write about. They give insights into how particular towns and villages developed, they describe the architecture of streets and buildings, and they discuss the lives of famous people who lived there. But however knowledgeable our authors are, the story they tell is necessarily incomplete.

Frith's photographs are so much more than plain historical documents. They are living proofs of the flow of human life down the generations. They show real people at real moments in history; and each of those people is the son or daughter of someone, the brother or sister, aunt or uncle, grandfather or grandmother of someone else. All of them lived, worked and played in the streets depicted in Frith's photographs.

We would be grateful if you would give us your insights into the places shown in our photographs: the streets and buildings, the shops, businesses and industries. Post your memories of life in those streets on the Frith website: what it was like growing up there, who ran the local shop and what shopping was like years ago; if your workplace is shown tell us about your working day and what the building is used for now. Read other visitors' memories and reconnect with your shared local history and heritage. With your help more and more Frith photographs can be brought to life, and vital memories preserved for posterity, and for the benefit of historians in the future.

Wherever possible, we will try to include some of your comments in future editions of our books. Moreover, if you spot errors in dates, titles or other facts, please let us know, because our archive records are not always completely accurate—they rely on 140 years of human endeavour and hand-compiled records. You can email us using the contact form on the website.

Thank you!

For further information, trade, or author enquiries please contact us at the address below:

The Francis Frith Collection, Oakley Business Park, Wylye Road, Dinton, Wiltshire SP3 5EU.

Tel: +44 (0)1722 716 376 Fax: +44 (0)1722 716 881
e-mail: sales@francisfrith.co.uk **www.francisfrith.com**